Barefoot Muse
PRESS

High-Voltage Lines

High-Voltage Lines

by
Tiel Aisha Ansari

Barefoot Muse Press
2012

First edition, 2012
Published by Barefoot Muse Press

ISBN-13: 978-0615663760
ISBN-10: 0615663761

Printed in the United States of America

ACKNOWLEDGMENTS

"The Nightingale, the Rose, and What Came After," "A Postcard Full of Sky," "Lamia on Keats," and "Silent Witness Train" inspired by Neil Gaiman, author of *Sandman*.

Previously published:

"Lines on Notes on Lines" *The Ghazal Page*, 2012

"Faust in the Industrial Age" *Raintown Review*, 2009

"Hobo's Door" *The Road Not Taken*, 2009

"Fluid Boundaries" *Villanelles*, anthology, Everyman's Library Pocket Poet series 2012

"Roomba" *Tilt-a-Whirl*, 2012

"Leavened Bread" *Scribblers on the Roof*, 2009

"Funeral Home Coffee" *Raintown Review*, 2009

"Edgar on Time" *The Lyric*, 2009

"Penelope" *The Lyric*, 2009

"Your Karma Ran Over My Fox" *Raintown Review*, 2010

"Up" *Barefoot Muse*, 2010; *Best of the Barefoot Muse*, anthology, Barefoot Muse Press 2012

Contents

The Author Introduces Herself

Phrenologue dialogue:
Doctor O'Quackery
says that my cranium
shows I am dull.

Lethally boring, the
un-entertaining-est
gal in the world, by the
bumps on my skull.

Solstice Light

All night I tossed and turned with dreams of light
and woke with early morning's gleams of light.

Remember how, in summer's darkless days
we woke and slept in blazing streams of light?

But winter swallowed up my memories
of light, digested them to memes of light

that sparkle in my tumbled-blanket thoughts
as dust motes dance in falling beams of light.

Solstices suspend the year, a crown
of days that hang between extremes of light.

Basso profundo, treble flute: the tones
that frame a symphony on themes of light.

The year falls ragged from my windowsill.
God hems the sky with silver seams of light.

Superdelegates

In superdelegates, that select group,
we find tomorrow's headlines. AP's scoop:
another one committed. Few remain
and each is duly courted by campaign
officials glad to jump through any hoop.

A vote in hand is worth two in the coop,
and as these birds fly home, the losers droop
while winners pat their backs and count their gain
in superdelegates.

Who are they anyway, this oddball troop
of party stalwarts, people "in the loop"
who'll make or break the nominee? Explain
before you pop that victory champagne,
how chosen, and by whom? Who put the *soup*
in superdelegates?

The Nightingale, the Rose, and What Came After

"If you want a red rose," said the Tree, "you must build it out of music by moonlight, and stain it with your own heart's-blood."—"The Nightingale and the Rose" by Oscar Wilde

The nightingale is dead. The perfect rose
that blossomed crimson as a tongue of fire
dissolves the coolness that is her pose,

unleashes unacceptable desire.
She wants a doggy tongue between her thighs
to blossom crimson as a tongue of fire.

He plays her pet. It comes as no surprise
that dominance and bondage are her games,
that she wants doggy tongue between her thighs.

She puts a rubber collar on him, names
him Fido—fit name for a canine stud,
for decadence and bondage are her games.

She takes the gift he brought, the rose of blood,
inserts it in the rubber collar's notch,
"Here, Fido," fits it on her canine stud.

He doesn't care, while nosing at her crotch,
the nightingale is dead. The perfect rose
inserted in the collar's final notch
destroys the coolness that was her pose.

Lines on Notes on Lines

What disciplined care composers devote to their lines
when passion would scatter black and white notes from their lines!

Feet shuffle dusty roads in the dawn, drawn
by the swinging of chapel bells in their cotes, on their lines.

The words of the duet are tragic; love, loss and despair
but the singer's voices distill ecstasy, remote from their lines.

Wind keens in the bay, flute over rhythm section:
slap of waves and creak of rocking boats at their lines.

Invisible panpipes echo from rocky, untenanted hills.
No-one is there to dance but tethered goats on their lines.

Have you heard my people singing the old freedom songs
as they stood in the rain, waiting to vote, in their lines?

Perched on the glass insulators atop a telephone pole
a meadowlark spills music from his throat down the lines.

Old women at sunset, faces wrinkled as dried apples
hum soft ballads, the stories that life wrote in their lines.

Drunk on the lyrics of Hafiz and Yunus, I make
a song to praise God out of quotes from their lines.

Walking Underwater

This morning's light was so intensely blue
it was like walking underwater. Each
day brings us a little more of day.

I found myself incapable of speech,
half-dazzled and half-drowned, a fish on land
this morning's light was so intensely blue.

As I lay gasping on the daylight strand
a dreamer hauled from sleep too fast to wake
I found myself incapable of speech.

What hook had caught me, what strange sportsman's take
I was, I could not know or even guess
as I lay gasping on the daylight strand.

The nights grow shorter now. I wake and bless
the sun's return, the promise of the year.
What hook had caught me, what strange sportsman's take—

awake, I laugh at dreamers and their fears.
This morning's light was so intensely blue
with sun's return, the promise of the year.
Each day brings us a little more of day.

Goodwill

My closet relies on the goodwill
of strangers. I dress in donations—
recycled from fashionable landfills
my closet relies on. The Goodwill
resells them and trains folks in job skills
at many convenient locations.
My closet relies on the Goodwill.
I'm dressed up in strangers' donations.

A Postcard Full of Sky

A postcard full of sky. How odd a thing
to sell: no rainbows, birds upon the wing
or even colored clouds. Just plain and blue,
serene—or maybe vacant. Tell me who
would think it was appropriate to ring

a tongueless bell to call a christening,
or come with laryngitis to a sing-
along? It seems offensive, sending you
a postcard full of sky.

I take it from the rack, considering
a figure-ground exchange, an opening
of eyes to subtler shades. I see it true:
a heaven infinite, unwritten, new.
Next time I see you, love, I think I'll bring
a postcard full of sky.

Sources of the Nile

Speke and Burton ventured up the Nile
to seek its source. They quarreled on the Nile

among the fever-trees and lion's dens,
the tropic grasslands that surround the Nile.

It's every pilgrim's dream to find the source
of something—maybe smaller than the Nile

or than a breadbox—still, a worthy goal.
But dangers line the edges of the Nile,

as these adventurers had found out. Pride
can dog your footsteps all along the Nile

with crocodile teeth and stinking breath.
Do not imagine you can claim the Nile

as *your* discovery. It's been there since
before you looked at any map. The Nile

will be there long after you're gone. Remember
you're not here to find and name the Nile,

but witness to the strength of water. Drink
and praise God for the beauty of the Nile.

Faust in the Industrial Age

The fire-escape is faulty. Do ascend
with care; don't stomp and shake it loose. The noise
would wake the neighborhood, and people tend

to like their sleep. Each ashen dawn destroys
some dreamer's childhood home of hedgerows
where sparrows hide their nests from egging boys

and girls weave daisy-chains and tie bright bows
in feathered bangs. Nostalgia is the lot
of country mice who've stuck their furry toes

in city traps. But you and I are not
of such a breed; we're alley cats. So come,
survey our designated kingdom from this spot,

this warehouse roof, so high beneath the dome
of sky defined by traceries of smoke,
the ceiling of the place that we call home.

It's midnight, but the witching-hour stroke
will go unstruck tonight. The clock is dead,
its restless hands are still. The mainspring broke

when you and I walked past, our timeless tread
too heavy for that slave of Time to bear.
We've silence for the things that must be said.

But claim your power, and the very air
will veil your limbs in roiling clouds of soot
and carry you invisible to where

your mousy minions cower underfoot.
At your word, every door will stand unlocked
and every window open, spilling loot

while merchants flutter helplessly and shocked
consumers turn from reading Vogue *and* Trend.
You'd never find a route to freedom blocked.

This city your fief, world without end:
but trust in Mephistopheles, your friend.

New York Minute

I knew it instantly; the light had turned.
The driver in the car behind, concerned
leaned on his horn, as if he thought me sleeping.
I don't drive fast, it's true: some call it creeping.
I'm not a speed freak, that's all. I've not earned

disapprobation on this scale. I've learned
to take it easy, given up (or spurned)
commuter rat race. When I heard the beeping
I knew it instantly—

he was the type who usually returned
from drives with each last shred of patience burned,
nerves in a tangle and blood pressure leaping.
Unhealthy fellow: does he know he's keeping
time on clocks in courts that have adjourned?
I knew it instantly.

Hobo's Door

There are no trains that run here. Even so
the town aligns itself to unseen tracks
and every night I hear the whistle blow.

Our sons and daughters go and don't come back.
No-one talks about it, but we know
the town aligns itself to unseen tracks.

As in the sunset's dreamy afterglow
as when the dawn draws light out of the black
no-one talks about it, but we know

there's something out there, something that we lack
a thing half-light can only halfway show
as when the dawn draws light out of the black.

At midnight, vision's full. At midnight, go.
The hobo's door is open, just a crack
a thing half-light can only halfway show,

a thing that day will hide behind this fact:
there are no trains that run here. Even so,
the hobo's door is open, just a crack
and every night, I hear the whistle blow.

Lamia on Keats

Apprentice surgeon, student at the Guy
where he was dresser; where he caught my eye.
Something about his hands—his face—bespoke
perceptions more than normal.
                                    I awoke
his intellect, his passion. What a plan
I had for Keats, that troubled child of man!
Each day he labored underneath my sign:
caduceus of Hermes, wand divine.
I filled his dreams with serpents twined in pairs
like strands of protein helixed into hairs.
I made him mad with wanting Truth. The tools
for finding it were then at hand: the rules
of logic and experiment were known.
He worked his hands in blood and guts and bone
each day, deep-anchored in reality
and human need.
                        I meant for him to be
a leader of the coming generation:
seekers after knowledge who would fashion
vasty temples in the human mind.
His creativity, released, would find
cures for the illnesses that filled the Guy's
bleak corridors with pain and hopeless eyes.

You find it odd that I, a thing of Myth
would want to speed the march of Science with
a pair of hands like his? But genius
follows the Psychopomp's caduceus
wherever it may lead. I was his muse:
his field of expertise was mine to choose.
I looked ahead to ages that would name
my kin as legends, stories meant to tame
the ignorant chaos of the youthful race.

I saw that glory written on his face:
a torch to light the turning of the page
a hero of the new Promethean age!
I showed him how to read the saraband
of base-pairs on a chromosomal strand,
those variations infinite on cosmic themes.
These were the "Lamiae" that fed his dreams.
This secret, pregnant with revelation,
this model of divine recombination,
meiosis symbolized by twining snakes—
but see what use of it the poet makes!
He turns it to poetical caprice
with Science as the villain of the piece!

That's how he chose to write my story down:
John Keats, who could have garnered Darwin's crown.

Fluid Boundaries

Would I know you if I wore your mask
occupied the flesh you call your face
or is that something that I shouldn't ask?

I sip your essence from a full-lipped flask
a mouth against the wall of other-space—
but would I know you if I wore your mask?

Your wine is private; I would broach your cask
and swallow you in intimate embrace
or is that something that I shouldn't ask?

Smoke and water in my eager grasp
you penetrate me, leaving not a trace
so would I know you if I wore your mask?

You flow where I am dammed and filling fast
as I would fill your frame, invade your place
or is that something that I shouldn't ask?

Fluid boundaries define this task
of my imposing: edges to erase.
But would I know you if I wore your mask
or is that something that I shouldn't ask?

Roomba

To think you're still maintaining that old score
as if you were bartending, and my tab
was full of unpaid drinks. I swear you're like
a Roomba swooping round a polished floor
in search of any strand of lint to grab,
or vultures waiting for a car to strike

some sorry squirrel. "Justice is on strike",
you mutter, while your heavy hand is scoring
gouges in the tabletop. I grab
another can of beer and pull the tab.
It overflows and soaks the vinyl flooring
like the Red Sea drowning Pharoah. Like—

oh, who cares what the hell this beer is like?
It only counts as yet another strike
against me. Get the mop out, scrub the floor
and put it all down on my growing score.
You know I'll never live to pay this tab,
you'll have to settle for what you can grab:

unsatisfactory, I'm sure. It grabs
me, though I doubt it's to your liking,
that I should dodge the arrows, slings and stabs
of vast, outrageous fortune's random striking
and exit, leaving this unsettled score,
a steaming pile of grudge upon the floor

of your neat parlor. Truly, I was floored
to find you hadn't let it go. You grab
on, pit-bull stubborn. Slights are underscored
by constant replays that you treasure like
a has-been pitcher watching his last strike
on video. You won't erase the tab

of your old habits. Flip its power-tab
and Roomba buzzes mindless round the floor,
gets stuck in corners, never tries to strike
a new frontier. They programmed it to grab

what it runs over, good and bad alike.
Poor robot Roomba doesn't know the score.

You had to grab the mike, so take the floor
and call the strikes and runs just as you like.
There's no-one keeping tabs or taking score.

Southbound Train

Love letters lie in the rain
photographs float on the breeze
ink eddies dark down the drain.
Love letters lie. In the rain,
a slow-moving sad southbound train
leaves from the platform where these
love letters lie in the rain,
photographs float on the breeze.

Threshed

The combines leave the fields stripped and bare,
the straw all baled, the grain threshed into sacks
and sparrows search in vain for insects there.

The frosts will kill. The field-mice prepare,
collecting any trace of wheat or flax
the combines left. The fields, stripped and bare

are hazed with diesel fumes in dusty air
and though they hop and peck in tire tracks,
the sparrows search in vain for insects there.

Persephone in *déshabillé* despairs
of rising. Agricultural attacks
combine to leave the fields stripped and bare

and naked soil damaged past repair,
exposing roots that grope for what they lack
while sparrows search in vain for insects where

the farmers used to hold the Harvest Fair.
Then gleaners came, and carried bushels back.
Now combines leave the fields stripped and bare
and sparrows search in vain for insects there.

The Old Year, Unemployed

The old year departs, like an embittered
civil servant leaving office under a new
administration. His desk is littered
with crumpled papers that refuse to unfold:
the past is past. The sound of his shoe
dies away into the dark and the cold.

Where does a year go? Out in the cold,
down to the bar for a swallow of bitters,
a place he can rest, kick off his shoes
settle back and listen to the TV news.
Years are like sheep, they aren't born in litters.
There's only one at a time in the fold

like a single sheet in a manila folder
on a desk in an office that's growing colder
and colder. Once important, now just litter.
Is it any wonder the old year is bitter
feeling as useful as an unmatched shoe,
as any old thing replaced by a new?

The desk calendar says it's a new
year now. December has to fold
or be torn off. January steps into his shoe,
as months go, lighter but just as cold.
The old year's too worn out to be bitter
scuffing slowly through dead leaf litter.

The city will give you a fine for littering
but it's not a crime to make room for the new
by throwing out the old. Embittering
to be disposable, isn't it? Fold
your coat tighter to keep out the cold
stay warm by dancing the soft-shoe

shuffle, if those tattered shoes
can stand the abrasion from street litter.
Why does the year have to change when it's cold?
Ah, but this is all old, old news:

last year slouching off under a trifold
umbrella in a wind that bites bitter.

The folds in his face are deep and bitter.
The sidewalk is littered with yesterday's news
and his worn shoes can't keep out the cold.

Leavened Bread

There isn't time for leavened bread to rise,
the soldier's fists are pounding on the door.
We wipe the crusts of sleep from sleepy eyes

and look around us, bleak but unsurprised:
"We have to go now." Wanting to say more—
there isn't time.
     For leavened bread to rise

there must be time. There must be peace. The sighs
of yeasty breath from tender loaves, before
we wipe the crusts.
     Now sleep, from sleepy eyes

in children's faces, runs away. The skies
are dark. We're full of doubt, but one thing's sure:
there isn't time for leavened bread. To rise,

oh God, to rise from bed and realize
yesterday's home is now a hostile shore!
We wipe the crusts of grief from sleepless eyes

and pack what we can bear. It must suffice.
Whatever else the future has in store
pray God for time, that leavened bread may rise
and we wipe crusts of grief from weeping eyes.

Funeral Home Coffee

The clink of spoons in coffee cups sounds hollow
at the reception at the funeral home
and bitter grounds are laced through the last swallow
like wax-worms burrowing through honeycombs.

At the reception at the funeral home
the shadows crawl from corners, fill the air
like wax-worms burrowing through honeycombs
or cobwebs hanging over dim-lit stairs.

The shadows crawl from corners, fill the air
around a head with unkempt hair as drab
as cobwebs hanging over dim-eyed stares,
as dingy sheets on mortuary slabs.

Around a head with unkempt halo, drab
discussions follow lines of old dissent
as dingy sheets on mortuary slabs
are changed by tears to faded cerements.

Discussions follow lines of old dissent
on bitter grounds. They trace through the last swallow
that changes tears to faded sentiment.
The clink of spoons in coffee cups is hollow.

In the Kitchen

In the kitchen, on the stove, the pot
of water bubbles; pans are getting hot
and fragrant steam is rising, while the cook
stands on the porch. She has an eager look,
the clock says half past five, it's on the dot

but he's not there. There's traffic—quite a lot
he must be late—or maybe he forgot—
she won't believe that, sits down with a book
in the kitchen.

The towels on the rail are tied in knots
by anxious hands; the bread already got
a little burned; the mugs are on the hook
beside the coffee; in the breakfast nook
a woman's crying for a man who's not
in the kitchen.

Edgar on Time

Edgar:
The gods are just, and of our pleasant vices
Make instruments to plague us:
The dark and vicious place where thee he got
Cost him his eyes.
Edmund:
Th' hast spoken right, 'tis true.
The wheel is come full circle, I am here.
– *King Lear Act V, scene iii*

Time's arrow bends, but doesn't double back
though corkscrew curves may captivate your eye
and make you think you've retraced an old track.

So Edmund's wrong (as usual). He and I,
entwined like vines in sibling rivalry—
in corkscrew curves that captured both our eyes—

once walked this path, in immaturity,
boys playing bandit, robbing eggs from nests
entwined in vines. Our sibling rivalry,

inconsequential, never laid to rest
grew monstrous as we grew. We are no longer
boys playing bandit, robbing eggs from nests

but men commanding men. As we grew stronger
our hatred flourished, and its consequence
grew monstrous as we grew. We are no longer

children squabbling in our innocence
though all our actions retrace the old track.
Our hatred flourished, and its consequence:
Time's arrows loosed can never be called back.

Kyron

Kyron Horman disappeared near Skyline Elementary School June 4, 2010. His whereabouts remain unknown.

We're afraid to walk alone on Skyline Boulevard
where the trees reach up high and the canyons are deep.
Parents keep their children close to the yard
and stand guard on the stairs while the youngsters sleep.

Where the trees reach up high and the canyons are deep
a boy disappeared with no witness or warning.
They stand guard on the stairs while the young are asleep
but he vanished from school in the middle of morning.

A boy's disappeared without witness or warning.
Grim-faced men search the forest for traces of a life
that vanished from school in the middle of morning.
No-one saw a car pass and no-one smelled a knife.

Grim-faced men search the forest for any trace of life
hoping against hope to not find him dead.
No-one heard a car, no-one remembers a knife
like a claw digging into a face that fled.

Hope against hope that the lost is not dead,
but we no longer trust that hope does any good.
Despair digs its claws in the faces that led
the furious search in the wind-shaken woods.

We can no longer trust that it does any good
for parents to keep children close to their yard.
Now the Furies course the wind-shaken woods
and fear walks alone on Skyline Boulevard.

Destruction Psalms

A searing wind. A trembling leaf
that whispers a destruction psalm.
A roaring like a distant train,
the stealthy footfall of a thief,
the stirring of a weathervane,
a flake of ash falls on your palm.

You saw it on the news: the palms
in silhouette, with upraised leaves
like hands that prayed, but all in vain.
The flames spelled out destruction psalms
across the hills. They ran like thieves
in scarlet, fast as midnight trains.

What follows in disaster's train:
the desperate hold out their palms
and neighborhoods are stalked by thieves
while honest folk are forced to leave.
The music of destruction psalms
fills every heart and every vein.

A fallen, melted weathervane
points nowhere north. The bonfire train
whose whistle sang destruction psalms
whose breath burned hot as lit napalm
reduced to ash each living leaf.
Prometheus, you ancient thief

did you foresee this when you thieved
the sun for us? Was it in vain
you saw our promise and believed
that we could learn, we could be trained—
I bend my head. I fold my palms
I pray some more destruction psalms.

You ask the meaning of these psalms,
but ask the name of him, the thief
who set the fires among the palms.
Cruel, foolish, mad or vain?

The consequences now entrain
as trees unfold to withered leaf.

My veins are cryptic; reading palms
will leave no clues about the thieves
who train us in destruction psalms.

No Safe Harbor

Drifting is easy. Anchoring is hard.
In either case, safe harbor is denied me.
I drag my shackle round the prison yard.

They said early release was in the cards
if I learned to keep the anger all inside me.
But I've drifted free, and anchoring me is hard

on a sandy seabed. Always on my guard
against the free tongue that damned, hands that tied me,
I drag my shackle round the prison yard.

Anyone can claim their voyage was ill-starred.
I can't even blame the cruel eyes that spied me
drifting at ease. They drove my anchors hard

into cold concrete, under windows barred
with black iron crosses on which men have died. Me,
I drag my shackle round the prison yard.

Naked, I bear the jailer's indifferent regard.
These steel walls confine but cannot hide me.
Drifting was easy. Anchoring is hard.
I drag my shackle round the prison yard.

Silent Witness Train

A train of silent women rumbles through the night.
They do not speak. They do not move. They stare ahead
like statues waiting for museum staff to write
"A train of silent women rumbles through the night"
upon a plinth, around a painting's frame. They might
be ghosts. They might be refugees. They might be dead
or lost in space-time. Child or crone or maidenhead,
they do not speak. They do not move. They stare ahead
like eyeless skulls that watch from shadows under beds.
Like every silent witness dead of love or fright,
they do not speak. They do not move. They stare ahead,
the train of silent women rumbling through the night.

Penelope

Penelope, Ithaka's lonesome Queen
is weaving webs of excuse and deceit
to blind and bind the suitors she has seen
come crowding to her door on hasty feet.

She's weaving webs of excuse and deceit
that she unravels every night, alone.
They crowd into her door on hasty feet
each morn, to find her work is not yet done.

And she unravels, every night alone.
No word of him has come from foreign coasts
and each morn finds her work is not yet done.
They quarrel over her with foolish boasts

and every day she has to give report:
"No word of him has come from foreign coasts,"
to louts who fill the hall and crowd the court
and quarrel over her with foolish boasts.

And every day she gives a false report
to blind and bind the suitors she has seen,
the louts who fill her hall and want to court
Penelope, Ithaka's lonesome Queen.

Your Karma Ran Over My Fox

Last night—this morning—someone speeding hit
a fox. I found him dying in the brush
where he had crawled, just inches from his dig.
I tried to get him to a vet, but he
repelled me with a sharp-toothed snarl, no quibble
but a rank defiance and good-bye.

The conference champion gets a first-round bye
and Golden Globes are granted to a hit
TV show (are they biased? Let's not quibble),
while commissions are the Fuller Brush
man's earned reward. Each man receives what he
deserves, they say—it's karma, can't you dig?

So cosmic justice says that I should dig
a grave for this poor fox? And by the bye,
about that reckless driver—doesn't he
get karmic tickets for the fox he hit?
A glancing blow, it's true, a sidelong brush—
but still, the fox is dead. That's just a quibble.

And "unintentional?" Just one more quibble.
The careless comment and the vicious dig,
the calculated cut, the casual brush-
off, both draw blood. Each long-drawn-out good-bye
begins with blindfold darts, that *somehow* hit
the mark. He pled his innocence, but he

knew better all along. Like lawyers, he
reduced the heart of matters to a quibble
knowing he did damage with each hit.
The deepest traps are always those we dig
ourselves; our authorship gives us no bye
and self-made pitfalls hidden in the brush

are lethal as the arsenic on the brush
that Monet, absent-minded, licked while he
recorded emerald green impressions.
                                        Bye.
I've no time for your everlasting quibble.

Leave me here alone and let me dig
a victim's grave for the poor fox you hit.

His teeth are hard, and gleam. No quibbler, he.
I dig black dirt to hide his orange brush.
It hits me hard to say the last good-bye.

Break Me My Bounds

"Break me my bounds and let me fly"—"A Career," Paul Laurence Dunbar, 1872-1906

"Break me my bounds and let me fly!" I heard
a carol from an egg. An unhatched bird
was singing of the boundless open sky
he knew was his by right. The will to fly
cannot be crushed in feathered things. The herd

may call a child's dream of flight absurd
and wean him on the pap of hope deferred
but chick or calf, you'll know him by his cry:
"Break me my bounds!"

In February's darkness, Death had spurred
to Dunbar's side. His vision was too blurred
by illness to perceive the hollow eye
that fell on him: Death said, "It's time to die."
But Dunbar only answered with this word:
"Break me my bounds."

Up

Where were you when the fires rose up?
Where is the image before it shows up?

Seeds are deep-buried, far from the light,
somehow the shoot germinates and knows up.

Where did the sundial's shadow disappear to?
Clocks wind down and a child grows up.

Tell me if you know the final answers
why stones fall and water never flows up.

Where has yesterday's caravan gone,
footprints hidden by the dust that blows up?

Shopkeepers shut their doors and windows
sun's going down and it's time to close up.

I am dust and a shadow walking
call me, Lord, as my spirit goes up.

Under the Rose

May Allah guard your secret.—Sufi blessing

I pitched my tent beneath the burning rose
where smoke and silence were my only friends,
and what I saw there, only Allah knows

and He will guard my secret. Simple prose
cannot reveal, through its too rigid lens
what filled my tent beneath the burning rose.

But lyric lines—at least so I suppose—
may faintly echo something that transcends,
for you to hear. (But only Allah knows.)

Then, if you join the company of those
who labor tireless toward Allah's ends
and pitch their tents beneath the burning rose

we'll smile a wordless greeting, and dispose
of useless verbiage that blurs and bends
the Truth we've glimpsed, that only Allah knows.

And thus our caravan of pilgrims grows,
who seek the Friend, in company with friends
who pitch their tents beneath the burning rose
and hear, in silence… only Allah knows.

Burn

They came for love, and love has made them burn
and roar and spin and tremble. Watch them burn

like candle flames the size of mountains. Turn
and turn again against the drums and burn

like solar flares, like tiger-eyes. They yearn.
They struggle, they surrender, and they burn:

a brilliant sillhouette, a feather-fern
of smoke across a staring eye, a burn-

ing scar, a crescent moon, the milky churn
of galaxies that spin and shout—*Praise God!*—and burn.

About the Author

Tiel Aisha Ansari is a Sufi, martial artist, and data analyst living in the Pacific Northwest. Her work has appeared in *Fault Lines Poetry*, *Windfall*, *Verseweavers*, *The Lyric*, *Masara*, and an Everyman's Library anthology, among others. Her poetry has been featured on KBOO, Prairie Home Companion and MiPoRadio and has been nominated for a Pushcart Prize. Her collection *Knocking from Inside* is available from Ecstatic Exchange. Visit her online at knockingfrominside.blogspot.com

Made in the USA
Charleston, SC
17 July 2012